Aldgedeslegh

a poem

Roger N Bloor

*To Angela
from
Roger N Bloor
Jan 2019*

All rights reserved.
This book or any portion thereof may not be reproduced or used in any manner whatsoever without the express written permission of the copyright holder except for the use of brief quotations in a book review.

First Printing 2018

Published by
Audley and District Family History Society

Copyright of Text © 2018 Roger N Bloor
Copyright of Artwork © 2018 Roger N Bloor

All rights reserved.

ISBN-13: 9781730810909

Dedication

To those who live on in our memories
and those who will hold ours

Murphy, Leo, Miles & Seren

Acknowledgements

The historical content of this poem relies on the following sources:

Robert Speake, Audley – An out of the way, quiet place, Department of Adult Education at Keele University (1972)

Robert Speake, Audley Parish Millennium 1000 -2000 AD, Audley Rural District Council (2000)

Cooke, William, 'Wilfred Owen's 'Miners' and the Minnie Pit Disaster', English: Journal of the English Association, 26 (1977), 213 -218

Staffordshire Advertiser 'The Murder in North Staffordshire', Saturday 17 August 1844

Blore Heath 1459, <http://www.bloreheath.org/> [Accessed 1 October 2018

Open Domesday Book, released under a Creative Commons BY-SA li, ([Accessed 1 October 2018], http://opendomesday.org/place/SJ7950/audley/

Advice on North Staffordshire Dialect kindly provided by Dr I K Bloor

Advice on historical facts kindly provided by Mr Clive Millington & Mr Robert Mayer of the Audley and District Family History Society

"... perhaps the life of the world is held together by invisible chains of memory and loss and love. So many things, so many people, depart! And we can only repossess them in our minds."
James Baldwin

Foreword

Audley is a small parish situated in the North West of Staffordshire, edging on to the Cheshire border. The author and historian Robert Speake described it as 'An out of the way, quiet place' [1]

No parish is free from its stories of death and misery, Audley is no exception, the underlying motives for the events recounted in this poem are universal and could be transported to any time and any place.

The poem addresses the ever-present spectre of Death who, residing at the parish bounds, readily accepts any invitation to visit, whether by the call of Lust, the pursuit of Power, the drive for Profit or the opportunity to renew acquaintance with his oldest friend Revenge.

The four stories within the poem shift through a dislocation of time, carrying with them the underlying link of untimely and violent death, the payment for the price of our imperfect humanity in an imperfect world.

---

[1] Robert Speake, *Audley*, (Keele: Department of Adult Education, 1972).

Aldgedeslegh

Aidley
Aldgedeslegh
Alderly
Audley
Audeley
Aldithley
Aldedeslega
Aldithelega
Aldedalega
Aldithlege
Aldithleia
Aldithelee
Auditheleg
Auddedelegh
Audedeleye
Audeyeleg
Aldithlegh
Aldgyp

*They conquer death
who live on still
within our memories*

- within our memories

High on this silent hill, look down at villages below
see churches, monuments and fields. Listen, hear the history –
sit quiet and walk in your mind those ancient paths and know

that this my friend – this is your parish, the parish of Aidley.
See the wheels, the spoil tips the smoke, look around
my son and see the coalfield heart of Staffordshire industry.

They say the King visited once, a lounge suit – passing through,
and Death my friend? – I'd say he knows his way here
well enough – no stranger to the parish bounds.

He knows the village name, the village ends, the shire's
boundaries, the village heart, the parish deeps and lands.
Death smiles when he speaks of Aldgedeslegh.

- Aldgedeslegh

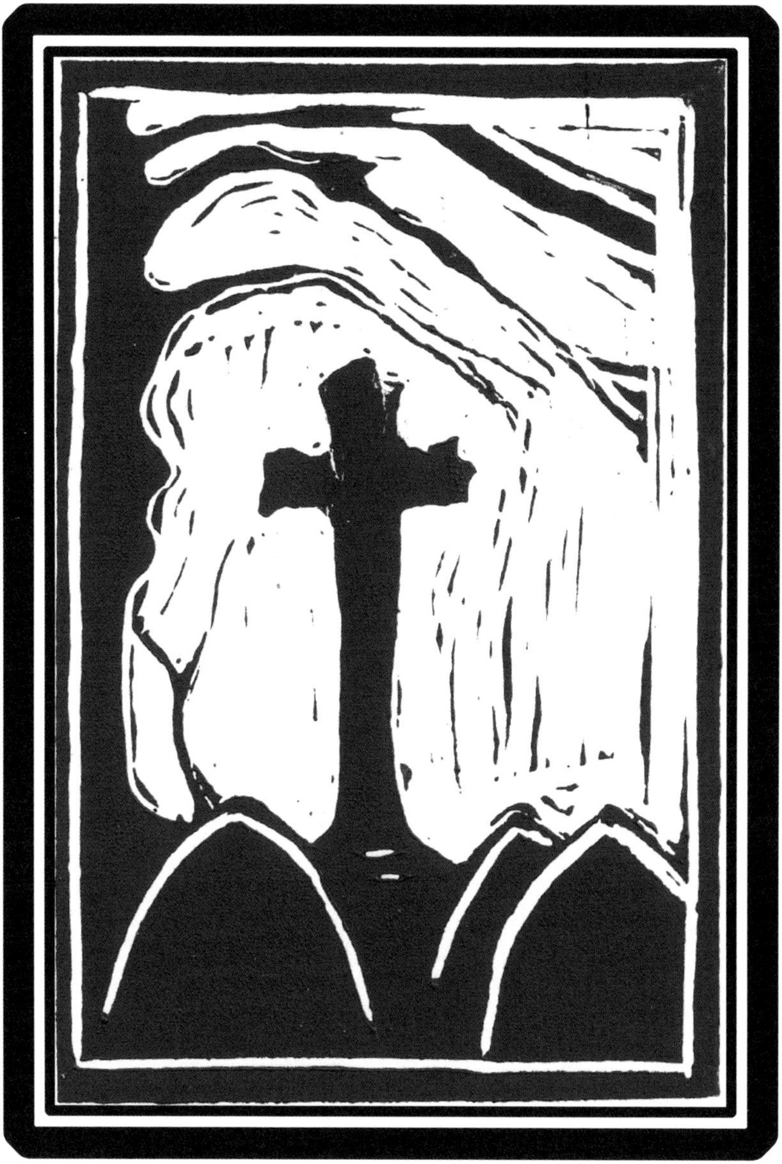

- Aldgedeslegh

This was how, in those Saxon times it was called,
how the village got that name, of course not now,
now they call it Aidley. But then, this ley was named

for the woman that they called Aldge, and this meadow
was hers, then after her Uluric and Godric, ceorls – but
freemen, turned off the land by Gamel the thegn, whose

Wergild was twelve hundred shillings worth, that
had no care for ceorls worth less than he,
no land no house no food no work – their fate.

His land you see here, half a hide, enough for three
ploughs not two, an acre of meadow, the wood yonder
a mile across? Maybe two that would be.

- Gamel the thegn

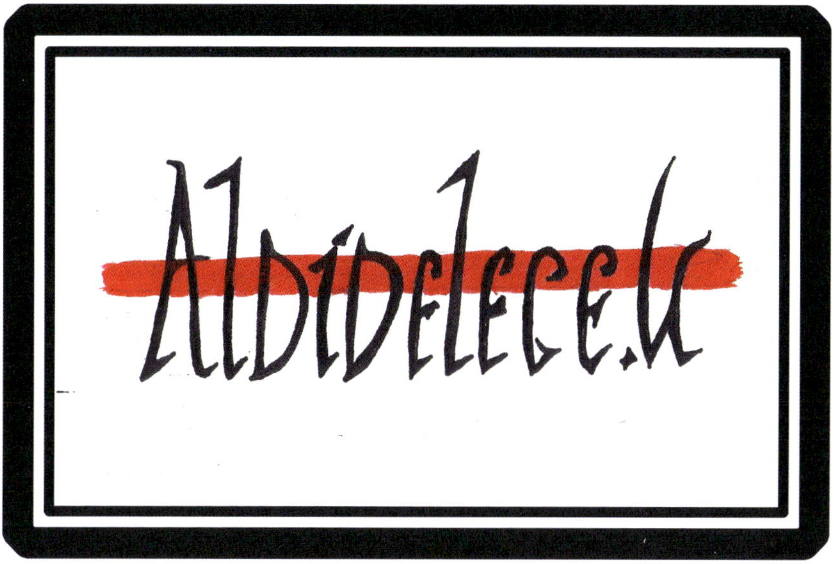

- Gamel the thegn

Property and wealth were not the least of Gamel's plunder,
he had no care for blood links, bible words or honesty
and in adultery did take his kinsman's wife and bedded her.

But knowing of his wife's unfaithfulness, Liulf of Alderly
father of Robert, crossed the Lime to find the lovers
and seeing her with Gamel sought revenge unlawfully.

Gamel in his passion, turned and saw his kinsman there,
come silent to this lonely place of Solomon.
His sword not drawn, could only watch the axe's fall.

So Liulf taking Gamel's life and land found fortune
for his sons and grandsons, the Lords of Aldithlegh, who
denying Saxon heritage created new their Norman name.

Took lordship of the villages, estates, the lands, and grew
their fortunes through royal patronage to be a dynasty.
The Lords of Audley – born from death and murder's due.

- the Lords of Aldithlegh

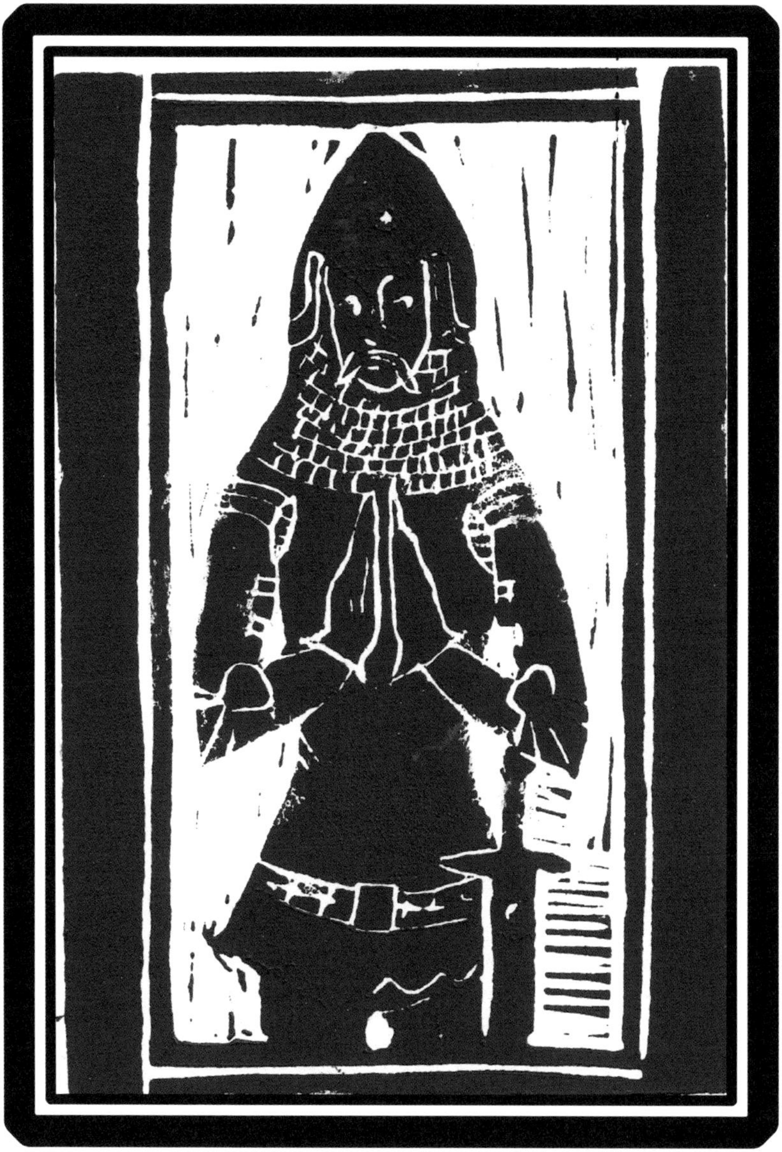

- the Lords of Aldithlegh

Next the Lords of Iron and Coal inherit power of industry
and rule. The owners of the land, the houses and the mines
creating new prosperity built on death and human misery.

The owners? – never seen – the Butty Men the Tommy Shops,
gave them all their profits – at a price we paid.
The price you ask? – poverty – injury – illness and deaths.

Listen now – down in the valley – the singing, the band parade,
it's 1885 – the opening of the Minnie Pit – a red letter day
in the annals of Audley mining, the owners and officials said.

- injury – illness and deaths

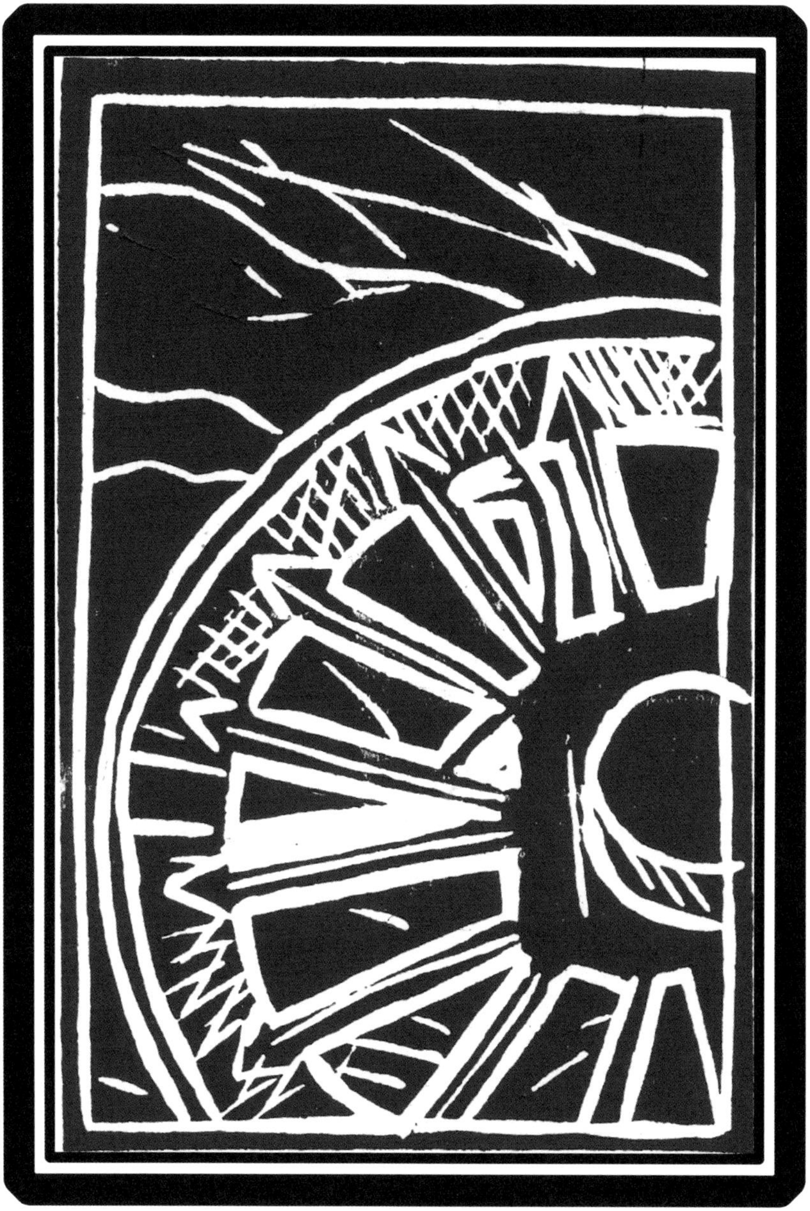

- injury – illness and deaths

Listen again, for the wind has blown the years fast away,
1918 – and in this last year of the Great War machine
the miners battle still with enemies of rock and clay.

9.45 in the morning of Saturday the 12th of January 1918
down in the seams of Bullhurst and Seven Feet Banbury
Death waits in the shadows of the shafts unseen.

Joseph Smith, the manager – in his office above pit three.
In the mine, two hundred and forty-eight mortal souls
dig coal, that murmurs in the hearth, but soon will sigh.

- but soon will sigh

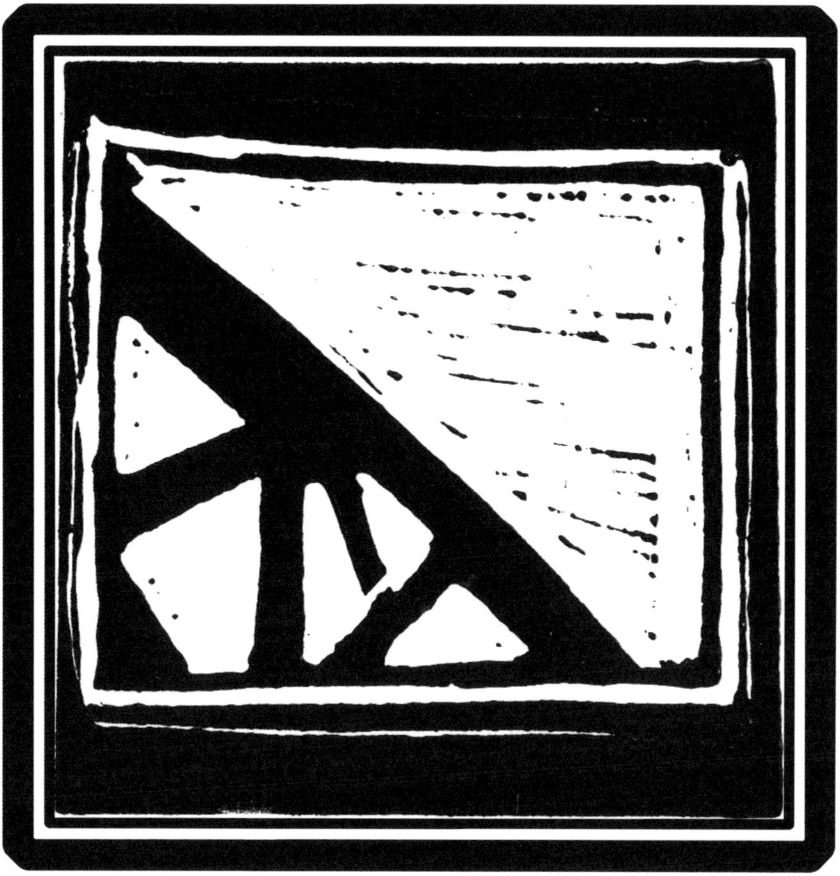

- but soon will sigh

They have this shift to go, then back to family, light and home
but deep within those seams – a single spark – from stone fall,
faulty lamp or firing shots was authoring their fate that hour.

The fire damp was the first to catch – then dust then coal
filling the shafts with gob stink death clouds,
explosions – taking down the roof – the walls.

- their fate that hour

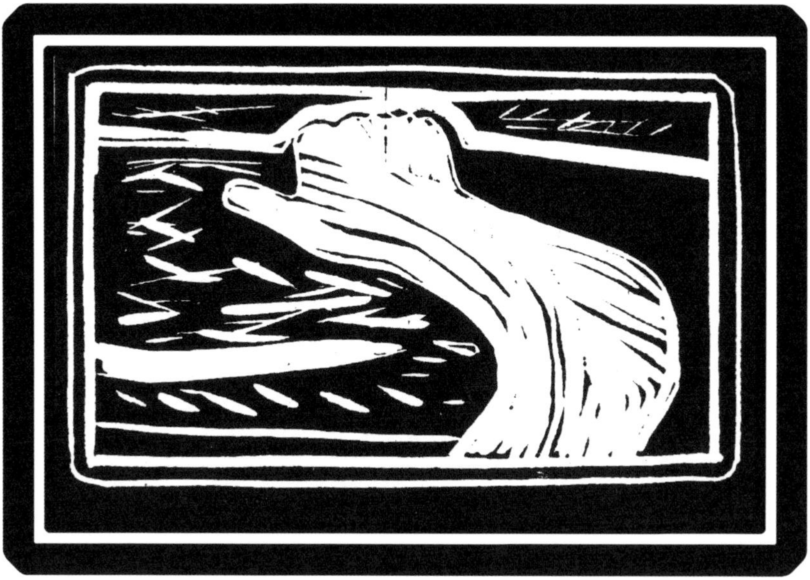

- their fate that hour

There was not to be a Hladik year, no silencing of sound
no stilling of the wind, no time for labour granted,
their atlas had no map of India that they should find.

That raindrop never fell, no shadows hung there halted,
pausing Death (who reads no novels – hears no prayer)
the shadow of Death moved fast – took life from all he passed.

One hundred and fifty-five men and boys died there
that day, one rescuer succumbing later to the foul air,
one hundred and fifty-six bodies for them to recover.

- Death moved fast

DISASTER.

MEN DEAD: ENTOMBED.

- Death moved fast

January 1918 – Scarborough – a hotel room by glowing fire
Wilfred Owen sits reading of the Podmore Colliery Disaster
the smoking coals rekindle memories of death and war.

He pens the lines of 'Miners' – next a letter to his mother
tells her that the piece is short but oh! – but oh so sour,
merges death of pit man with his dead and dark pit soldier.

The 4th of November 1918 5.45 am – France and zero hour
Owen leads his men under heavy fire – crosses the Soise Canal,
is killed – a week before the Armistice – no passing bells no choir

for him, who wrote of coals that sigh for earth beyond recall
of coals murmuring of their mine and moans of boys that slept,
of dying men who writhed for air and perished where they fell.

- memories of death and war

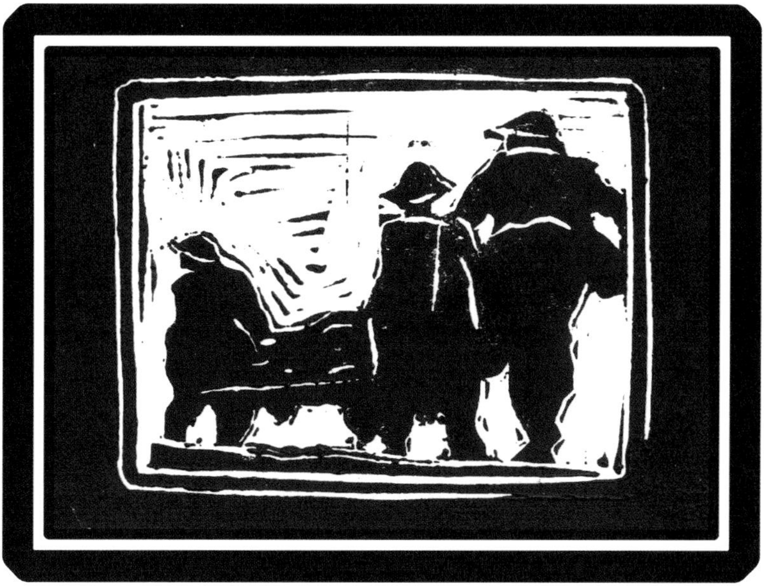

- memories of death and war

Margaret of Anjou – high in Mucklestone Church kept
watch on the battle fought across the heath. James Touchet
Lord of Audley, fighting for her cause, poised to intercept

the rebel army led by Richard Neville Earl of Salisbury
who heads for Ludlow, there to join a larger Yorkist force,
but first must fight the bloody battle of St Thecla's day.

September 23rd 1459 – two armies fighting for their cause,
Lancastrians, under Audley, set upon the shallow ridge
of Blore Heath's barren south west edge have paused

and wait in ambush, concealed behind the great high hedge,
with steep banked Wemberton Brook flowing fast below.
Listen now my son – hear silent prayer as fates converge.

- as fates converge

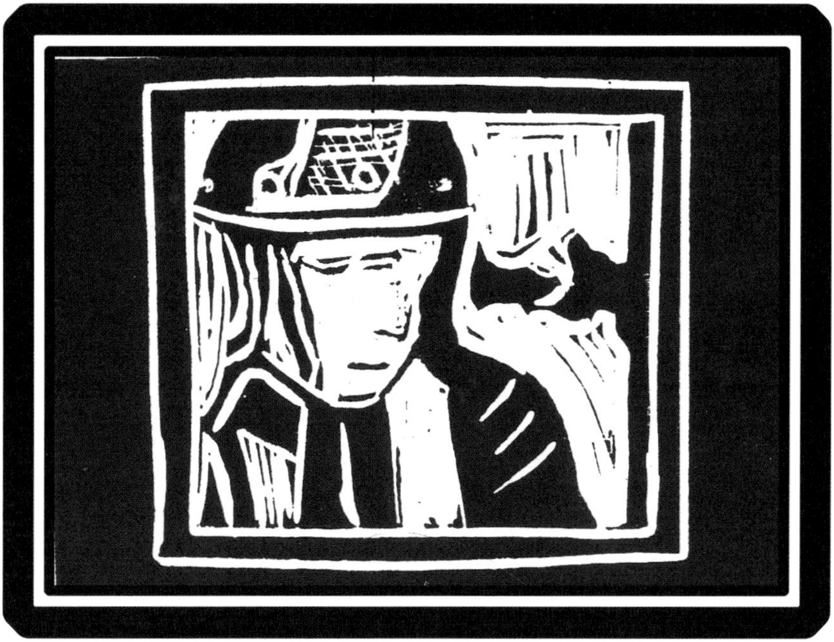

- as fates converge

Salisbury's men scouting land ahead saw banners hid low
to the west – an army part concealed – returned and warned
of Audley's strength – each Yorkist soldier matched by two.

Lord Neville sets his battle lines, right flank secured
by circled walls of carts – archers ranked to face the enemy
a furlong and a half away – the Brook providing safe divide.

The Yorkists sense defeat, kiss killing ground – for parley
twixt a rebel army and the king is certain doomed to fail
and battle soon will start with swarms of longbow archery.

Neville knows attack across the brook will not prevail,
withdraws his ranks of troops to feign a York retreat –
Audley sensing victory sends cavalry charging down the hill

to Wemberton's sloping banks – the Yorkists halt their flight,
the archers loose their bows and horses fall and riders die –
a second charge descends – the armies lock in bloody fight.

- certain doomed to fail

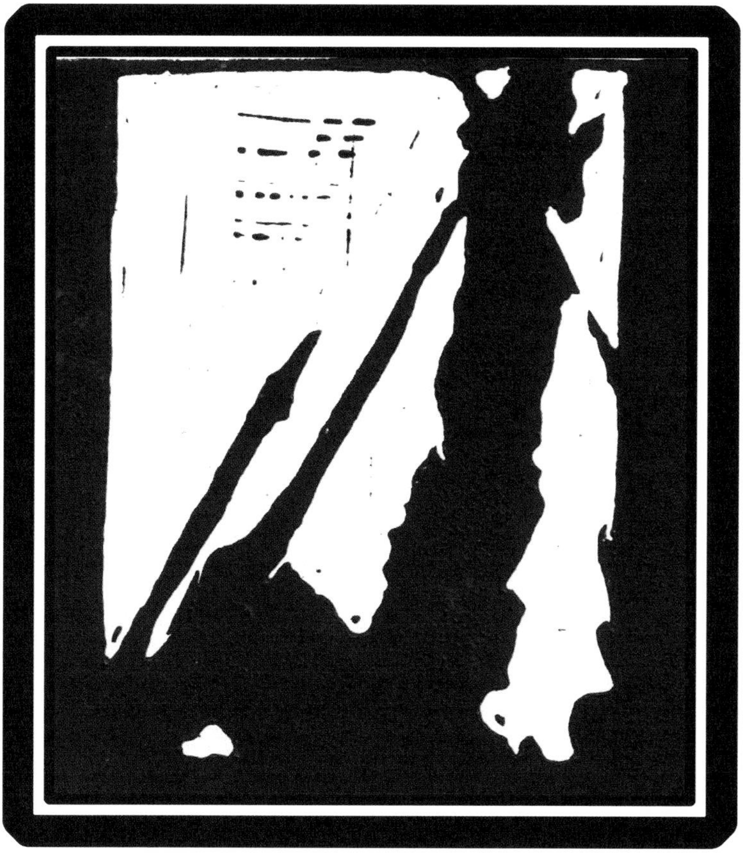

- certain doomed to fail

Sir Roger Kynaston finds Lord Audley in the deadly fray
and sword on sword they fight – until a single mortal blow
is struck and Audley fallen perishes upon St Thecla's day.

Their leader dead, the standard lost, Audley's men retreat
with Yorkists at their heels slaying all they find – leaving
dead and dying scattered wide across the bloodied heath.

For three days long the Brook runs red in mourning
but Margaret, sensing how the day was gone, has left –
her horse shoed backwards to disguise her leaving.

A cross upon the heath recalls the place Lord Audley fell,
but on that day three thousand loyal men had also died,
their death unmarked – they too have stories we should tell.

- stories we should tell

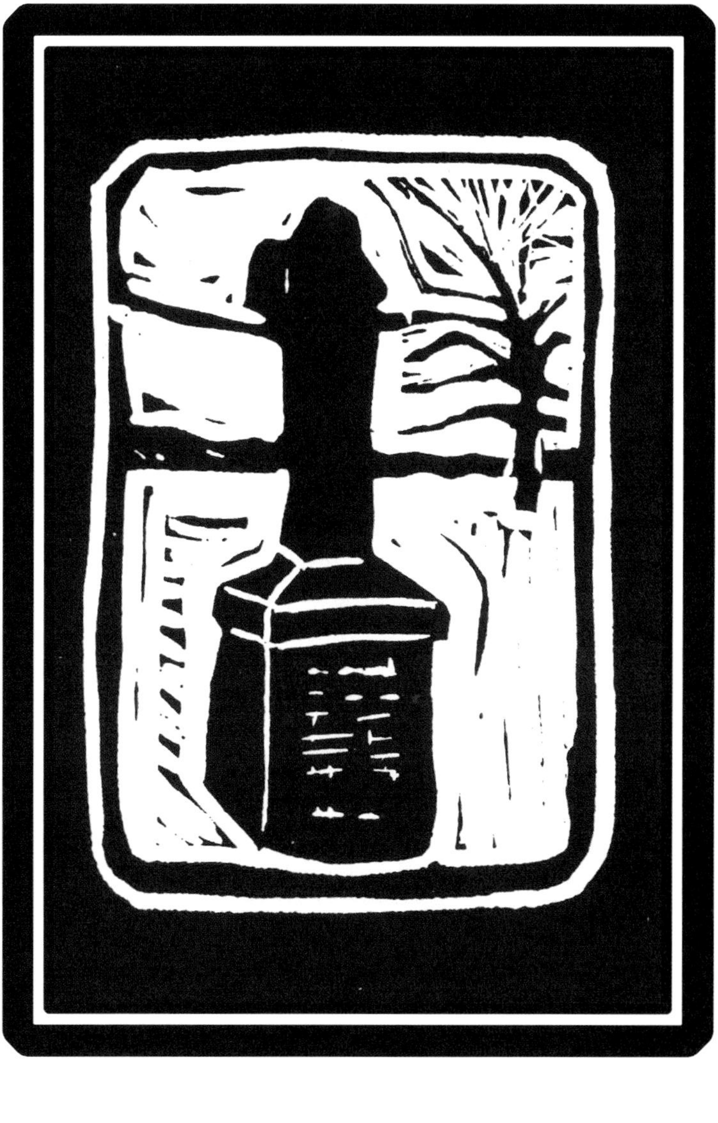

- stories we should tell

Sunday 4th of August 1844 "Pheasant 'Ayes – Weekes' Sundee Tom Cooper – gamekeeper ter Sir Thomas Boughey Bart, asleyp in bed, son William inna back frum goin' dine Aidley –

went theer fer chapel earlier in th'dee – met 'is mate an' ended up in th'Bowey Arms, then foer peynts at th'Kings and nar, near midneyght walkin' dine th'leene – wom leete."

He sees the cottage, walks towards the door – a shot rings out – he falls into the house, head on kitchen floor, blood pouring from his neck – his father rushes down and cradling

his son, shouts out to fetch a doctor fast – but William is dead, too late for help, his body lying half out the cottage door, his lungs awash with blood, carotid artery pierced – murdered

at the age of twenty-three – a melancholy and appalling case the papers said – the police were called and searched around the cottage grounds, found blue paper – wadding scraps

from where the gun was fired. Out in the yard they also found some shoe prints from a hobnail boot which had a pattern that they later matched with boots discovered at a suspect's house.

- a melancholy and appalling case

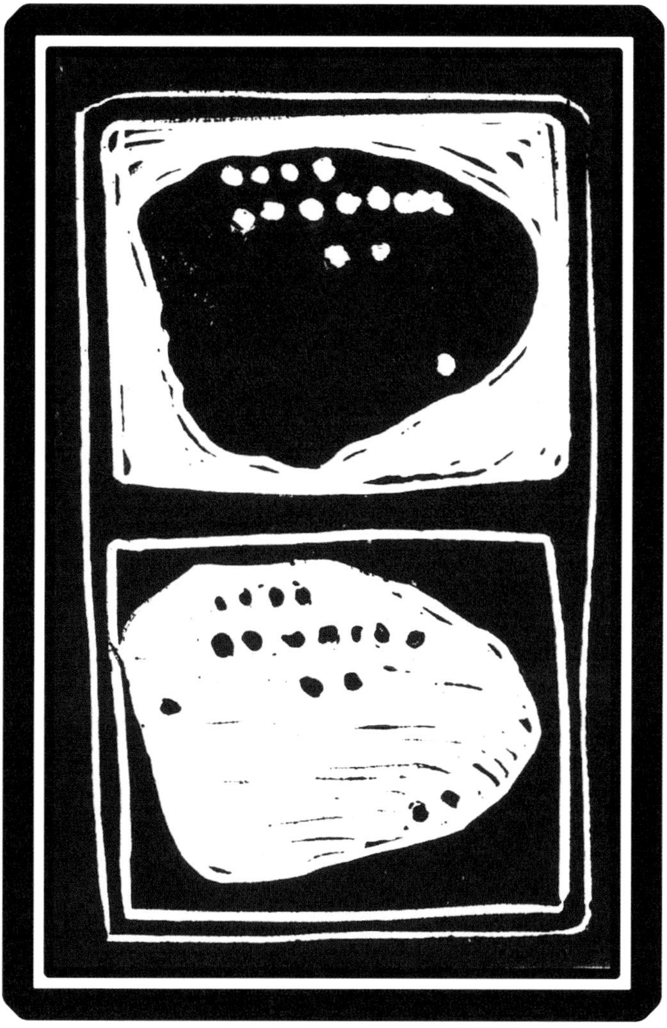

- a melancholy and appalling case

From information received the constables had made arrest
of local lad, Paul Downing, freed from gaol the previous day,
guilty of poaching on Thomas Cooper's evidence against

him. Downing claims, that Sunday night, he spent at Scot Hay
sleeping at Charles Powys' house, who would clear his name.
The police arrived at Powys' house and found there hid away

a gun – fired recently, and paper wadding, blue – the very same
discovered at the scene, Charles Powys taken into custody,
his boots removed and found to match the pattern in the lane.

Small things, but wadding paper and boot marks were to be
their downfall. Held for trial, a witness found, a young lad
Madders claims Downing uttered threats and heard him say,

after he was charged with poaching, "Ar'll wesh mey 'ands
in Cooper's 'art blud.", but no Christian name was mentioned.
The jury heard all the evidence and then the foreman

stood to give the verdict – said "guilty as they are charged"
but pleaded, as the lads were young, for mercy on their souls.
The judge, placing the black cap on his head, was not moved

- guilty as they are charged

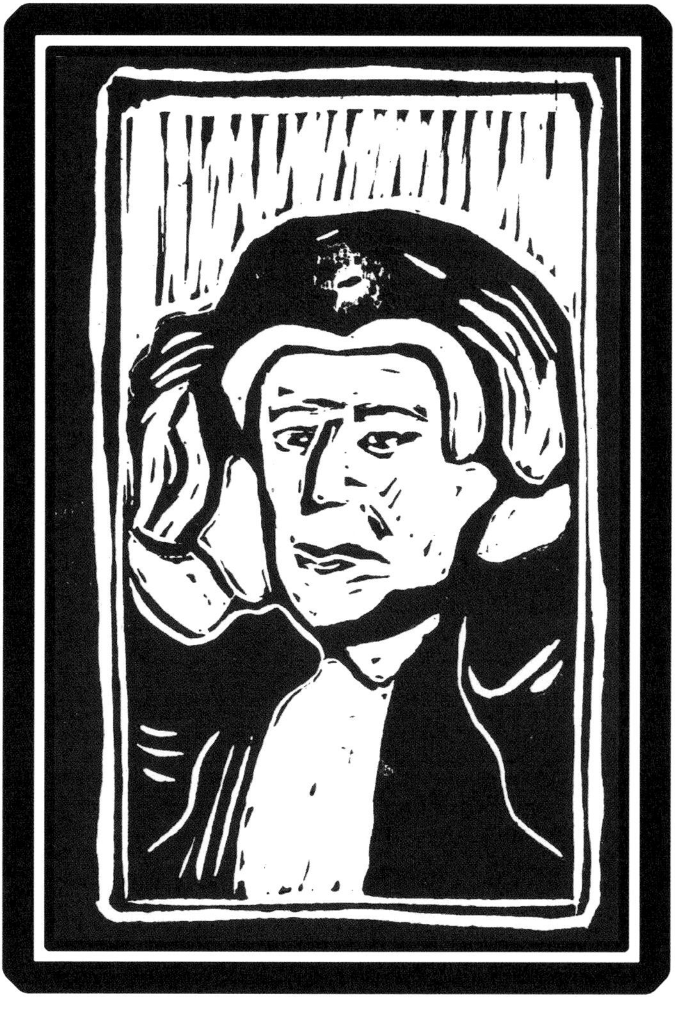

- guilty as they are charged

At noon, on January 25th 1845 the Stafford prison bell tolled the hour of their fate. The boys with warders and a priest were taken out to meet their end, upon the wooden scaffold

set outside the prison wall. Still protesting innocence Powys was heard to say "Weyn goin dey fer summat wey kneow nowt abite an' I 'ope th'Lord in 'eaven'll protect us."

Downing added "It'll be kneown afoer twelve month who's reyly th'guilty bloke, an' they'll bey now better off n'us.". Their final words now finished the nooses were in place and so

still engaged in prayer, the drop fell fast , and the world thus closed upon them for ever. A yeer later in a pub dine Ommerend a mon, drunk in a corner, were 'eard fer say – "Ere's the finger as pulled th'trigger wot shot Will Cooper dead."

- for whom the world has ever closed

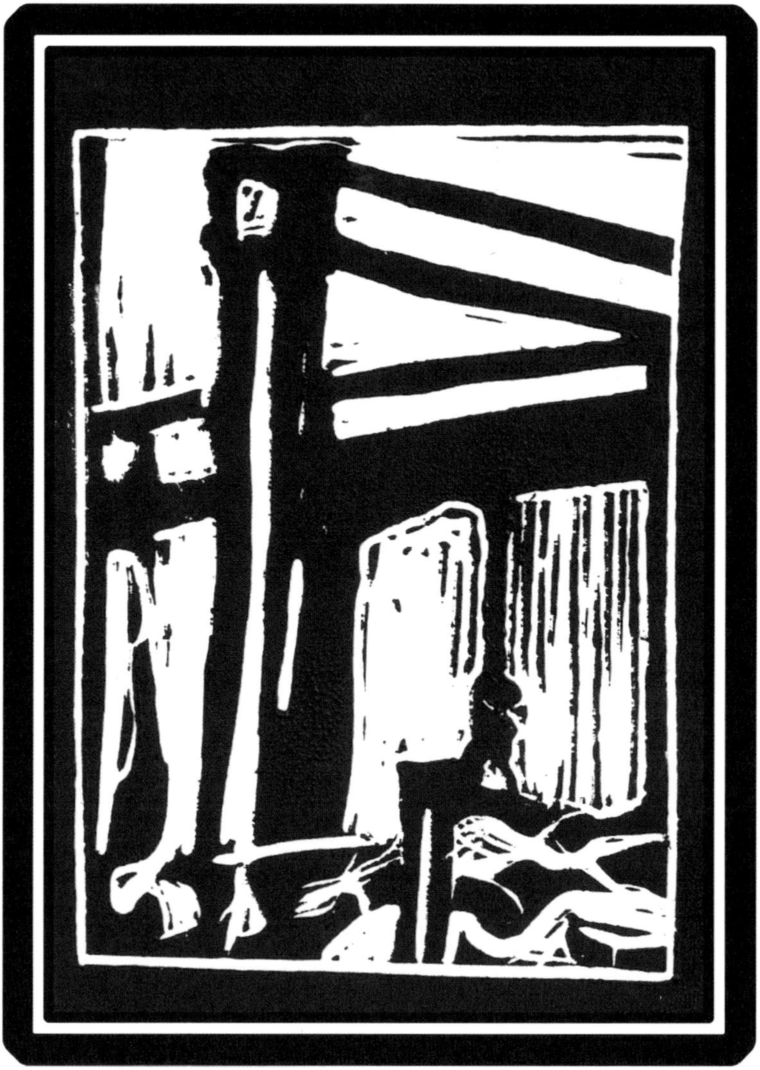

Postscript

In this place named Aldgedeslegh the glorious dead are now
remembered in our books, from Gamel the thegn,
to The Lords of Aldithlegh. But what of those who

knew enduring illness injury and death, do they remain
in memory, and in the darkness is their sigh, breathed
at the hour of their fate, heard drifting on the air again?

For them Death moved so fast their life outpaced
till only distant memories of death and war regale
the future from history written as their fates converged.

Each chapter of their story was certain doomed to fail
but still they leave their testimony for us to mind
of Death's triumphal melancholy – appalling tales

of lust, power profit and revenge, all guilty as charged.
They conquered death who live on still within our memories
those poor brave souls for whom the world has ever closed.

Notes

Page 12 Fire Damp is a flammable gas found in coal mines that accumulates in pockets in the coal and when they are penetrated the release can trigger explosions.

Page 12 Gob Stink is the odour from burning coal given off by an underground fire

Page 14 'There was not to be a Hladik year …' – Jorge Luis Borges, *The Secret Miracle*, a short story 1943

Page 28 'A yeer later in a pub dine Ommerend …' – A.Scott, *It meekes thee wonder*, A Centenary Compendium of Jabez Stories, 2015

Illustrations

Front cover design by the author

Front cover photograph by the author
(Chain on the Coal Wagon of the Minnie Pit Memorial)

Artwork by the author

Lino Cuts with Oil Based Ink
and Pen and Ink with Acrylic

Bibliography

Blore Heath 1459, <http://www.bloreheath.org/> [Accessed 1 October 2017].
Borges, Jorge Luis, 'The Secret Miracle', in Collected Fictions, ed. by Hurley, Andrew (London: Allen Lane, 1998), pp. 157 -162.
Cooke, William, 'Wilfred Owen's 'Miners' and the Minnie Pit Disaster', English: Journal of the English Association, 26 (1977), 213 -218.
Open Domesday Book, images released under a Creative Commons licence, ([Accessed 1 October 2018]).
Scott, A, 'It Meekes Thee Wonder,' in A Centenary Collection of the Jabez Stories, ed. by Bloor, R. Bloor, I. Bloor, A. and Bloor, D. (Newcastle under Lyme: AIRaD, 2015).
Speake, Robert, Audley (Keele: Department of Adult Education, 1972).
Staffordshire Advertiser 'The Murder in North Staffordshire', Saturday 17 August 1844.

The Author

Roger Bloor grew up in the village of Audley and went to school both at Audley and at Alsagers Bank. He is a retired consultant psychiatrist and former Senior Lecturer and Teaching Fellow at Keele University School of Medicine. Prior to his retirement he was the Lead for Medical Humanities at Keele University and has written poetry on and off for many years. Some of his writing is influenced by his experiences as a Royal Air Force Medical Branch psychiatrist and a specialist in Addiction Psychiatry, the remainder owes a great deal to life in general.

He is currently a student on the MA in Poetry Writing from Newcastle University studying at the Poetry School in London. He has a longstanding interest in history, and research and has written on significant folk from the past both in his poetry and other writings.

He has had poems published in The Hippocrates Prize Anthology 2017, Poetry Now Anthology '*Growing Old*', Allegro Poetry, Affect Publications '*StillBorn*', Words for the Wild Anthology 2018, Landscapes Anthology from Empress Press, The NHS 70th Anniversary Anthology, The Bridges Anthology and Magma Poetry Magazine.

His collection of Poems '*A Less Clear Dream*' was shortlisted for the Arnold Bennet Book Prize 2018.

He is Poet in Residence 2018/19 at the historic award winning Trentham Gardens in Staffordshire.

His Poetry webpages can be found **http://www.rogerbloor.co.uk/**

Printed in Poland
by Amazon Fulfillment
Poland Sp. z o.o., Wrocław